With
love
to
PHILIP,
an extra special member
of our precious human race

RUTH HELLER

WORLD OF LANGUAGE

MANY LUSCIOUS LOLLIPOPS

A Book About Adjectives

Written and illustrated by **RUTH HELLER**

PAPERSTAR

The Putnam & Grosset Group

An ADJECTIVE's terrific
when you want to be specific.
It easily identifies
by number, color or by size

TWELVE LARGE,
BLUE, GORGEOUS
butterflies.

It describes all things with style and grace...

and also it describes a place—

MYSTERIOUS, STAR-SPANGLED, ASTEROIDAL

outer space…

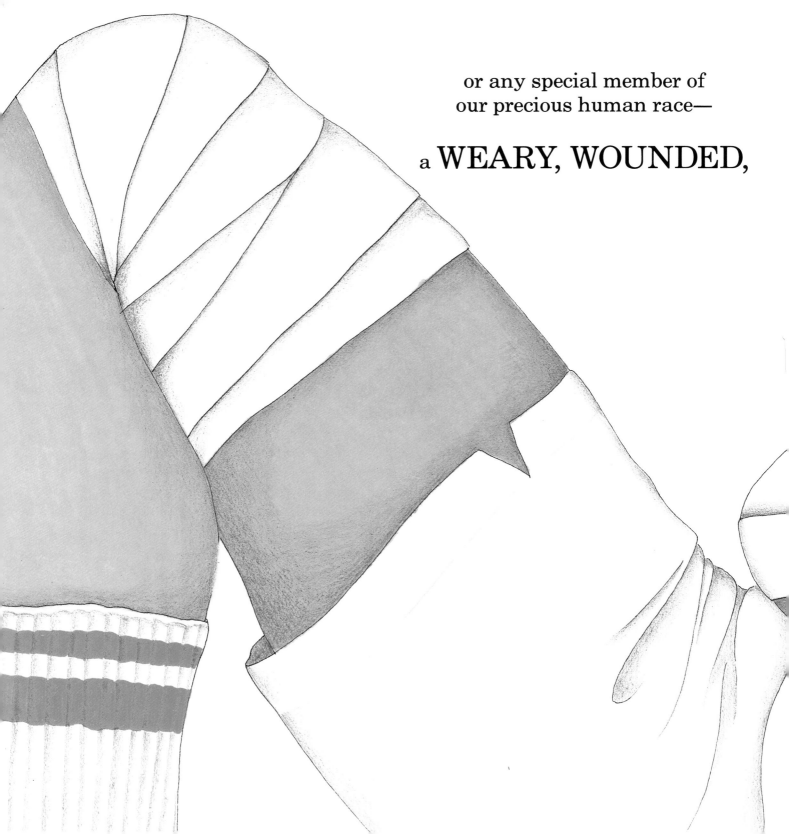

or any special member of
our precious human race—

a WEARY, WOUNDED,

BEARDED
and
BANDAGED
tennis ace.

An adjective describes a thought,
idea or emotion—

PEACEFUL coexistence,
a UNIVERSAL notion.

An adjective's terrific
even when it's not specific . . .

SOME jellybeans
a FEW gumdrops
and
MANY luscious lollipops.

It never fails
to
add details
to what
you
write
or
say…

a MESMERIZING,
COLORFUL and
GLITTERING display.

Use as many as you wish before,
but after
you need two or more…

A WET and SOGGY, DRIZZLY day,
RAINY, WINTERY and GRAY.

And it is perfectly okay
if you arrange your words this way—

Roses are RED.
Violets are BLUE.

They're PREDICATE ADJECTIVES
if you do…

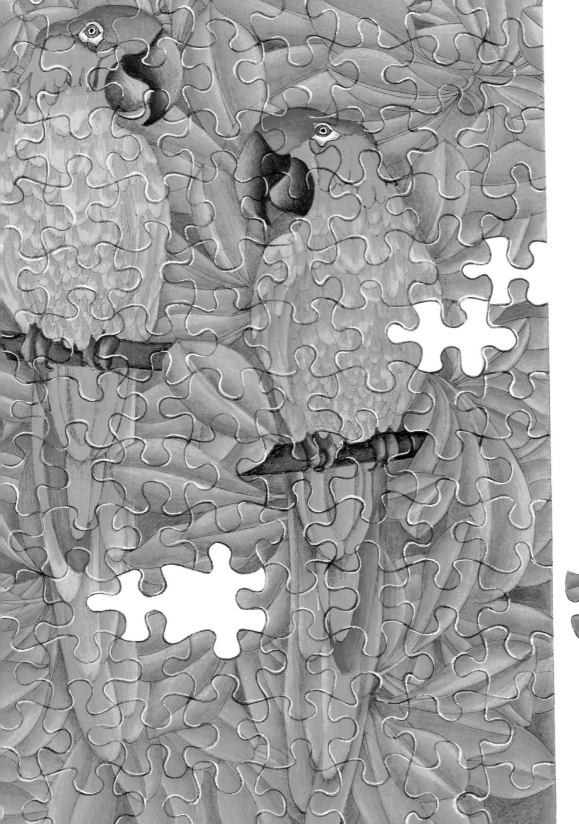

and
if you ask
a
question,
too—

Was
this puzzle
HARD
to do?

DEMONSTRATIVES will help you choose…

THIS way

THAT way

I like **THESE** socks
but
not **THOSE** shoes.

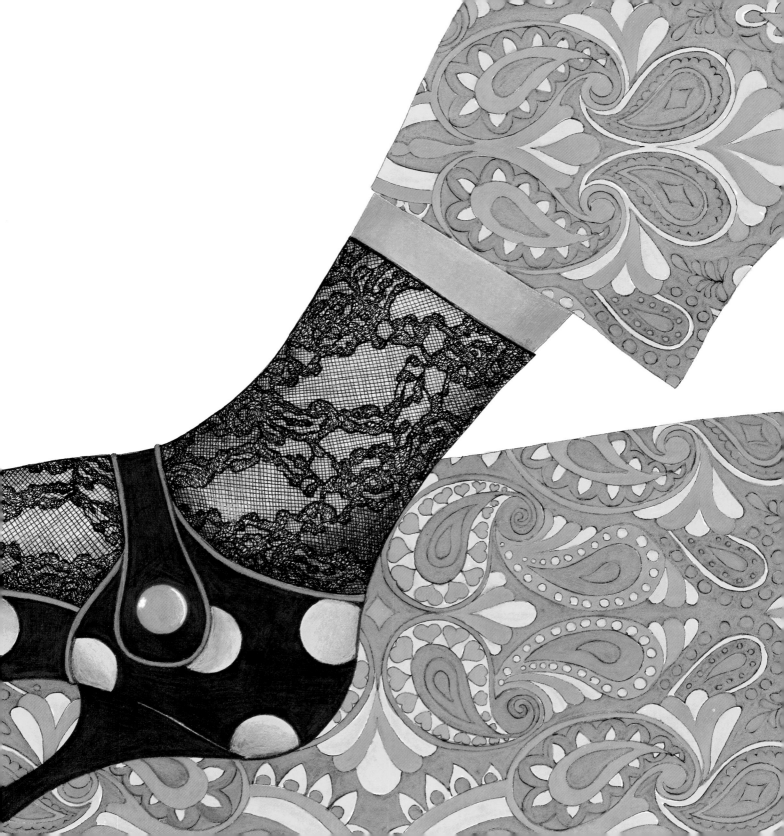

POSSESSIVES
always tell
you whose—

OUR
circus acts
are
front-page news...

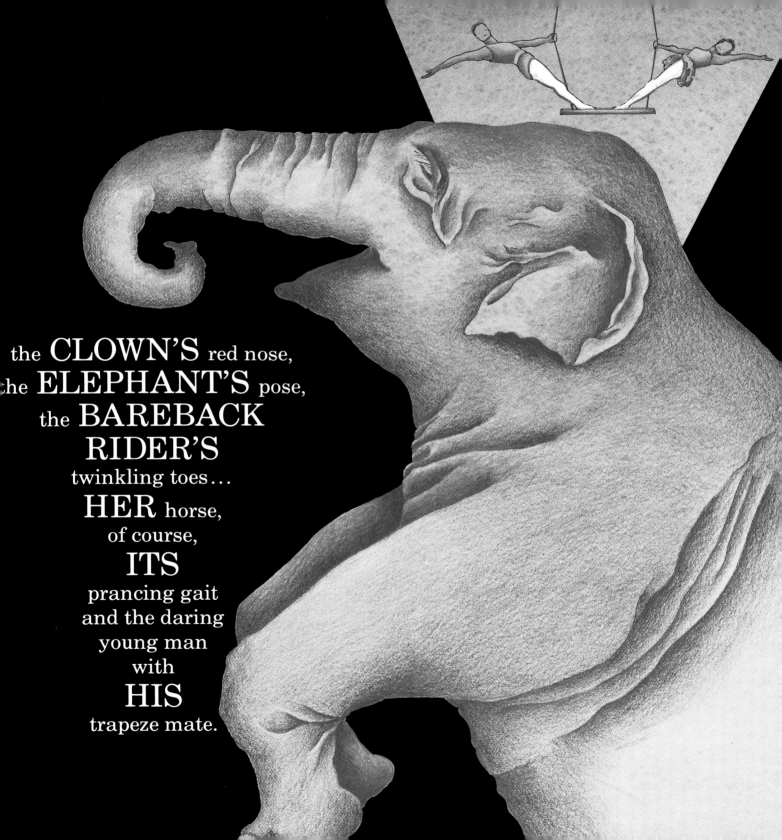

the CLOWN'S red nose,
he ELEPHANT'S pose,
the BAREBACK
RIDER'S
twinkling toes...
HER horse,
of course,
ITS
prancing gait
and the daring
young man
with
HIS
trapeze mate.

Three adjectives used frequently
are ARTICLES
A and **AN** and **THE**.

As anyone can plainly see...

there's **A** fern in **AN** urn on **THE** balcony.

Treat
PROPER
ADJECTIVES
the same
as any other
proper name…

a
PERSIAN
rug,
an
IRISH
setter.

They always begin
with a capital letter.

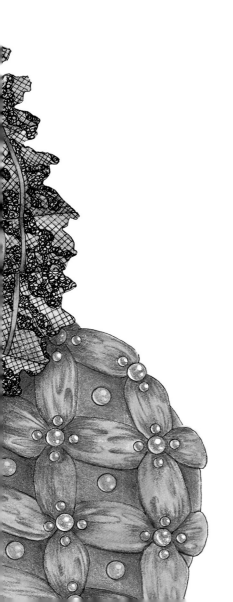

If you wish to create an adjective,
add
•IBLE or •ABLE or •OUS or •IVE
or any other suffix
seen
describing this
FAM•OUS,
REMARK•ABLE queen

with her DOLL•LIKE face
and GOLD•EN crown
and JEWEL•ED,
IRRESIST•IBLE
Renaissance gown.

It's a BEAUTI•FUL,
REG•AL,
EXPENS•IVE dress
for this popular monarch
called Good Queen Bess.

She has LOVE•LY,
SATIN•Y,
FLAW•LESS pearls
and GLEAM•ING gems
in her RED•DISH curls.

Some adjectives compare…

CURLY   CURLIER

FAIREST   FAIRER

CURLIEST hair

FAIR

For COMPARATIVES just add an •ER,
for SUPERLATIVES, an •EST,
except…

for the few IRREGULAR ones like…

GOOD and

BETTER

and BEST.

(See the back of this book for the rest.)

Use comparatives to compare just two
and superlatives for more.

The **TALLER**
animal of these two…

is the
TALLEST
one of the four.

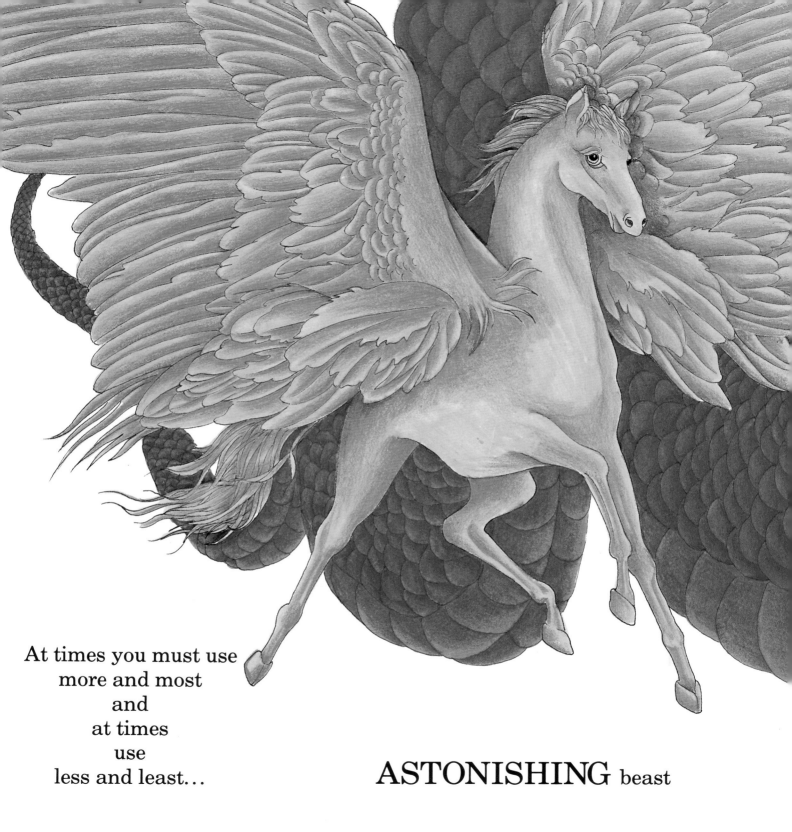

At times you must use
more and most
and
at times
use
less and least…

ASTONISHING beast

more
ASTONISHING beast

the
most
ASTONISHING beast

FATTENING
feast

less
FATTENING
feast

and the last
is the
least…

the
least
FATTENING
feast.

Is it most or more or least or less?
How do you relieve this alarming distress?

It isn't amusing. It's very confusing.
Which one of these words should you really be using?

Or should you just add an •ER or an •EST?
No one has yet found an infallible test.

But •ER and •EST are usually best
with words that have one syllable...

and also two if they end in Y
after you change the Y to I.

Three-syllable words and words with more
use less and least and most and more.

Here are some that work
both ways—either is correct.

able	polite
angry	quiet
clever	secure
friendly	simple
gentle	stupid
handsome	
narrow	
obscure	

Here are the irregular ones
I told you to expect.

bad	worse	worst
ill	worse	worst
little	less	least
many	more	most
some	more	most
much	more	most
well	better	best
far	farther	farthest

Whenever you find yourself in doubt,
be cautious and be wary.
It's often very helpful
to consult your dictionary.